The Heart Is Not a Pump

poems by

Aurore Sibley

Finishing Line Press
Georgetown, Kentucky

The Heart Is Not a Pump

Copyright © 2017 by Aurore Sibley
ISBN 978-1-63534-366-3 First Edition
All rights reserved under International and Pan-American Copyright Conventions. No part of this book may be reproduced in any manner whatsoever without written permission from the publisher, except in the case of brief quotations embodied in critical articles and reviews.

Editor: Christen Kincaid

Cover Art: Aurore Sibley

Author Photo: Aurore Sibley

Cover Design: Elizabeth Maines McCleavy

Printed in the USA on acid-free paper.
Order online: www.finishinglinepress.com
            also available on amazon.com

                    Author inquiries and mail orders:
                         Finishing Line Press
                            P. O. Box 1626
                      Georgetown, Kentucky 40324
                                U. S. A.

Table of Contents

1. The Farmer
2. Breakfast
3. Chocolate
4. Dog Park Romance
5. Soviet Delicacy
6. The Ox and The Dragon
7. Limerence
8. Clean Gone
9. Like the Sun and Moon We Both Can Shine
10. Oliver
11. Goethe's Theory of Color
12. Secrets of the Skeleton
13. The Way the Wind Sounds
14. Sailor Man
15. Flame in Seed
16. Artifical Light
17. Skylark
18. The Heart is Not a Pump
19. Playing Chopin
20. The Sunflower is a Twelve-pointed Star
21. Loss
22. Malignancy
23. One Was Not Enough
24. The Orange Clawfoot Bathtub
25. Lover's Point

The Farmer

It was the earth I fell in love with,
I swear it was.
It was the feel of the dirt clods crumbling
In my soft palms, the smell of
The hay and the sage and strawberry plants,
The sun glinting through the ocean haze, the fields
Rolling past like water running down a hill,
All glistening with wheat and grapevines,
It was the way the dust coated my jeans.

The earth is more fertile than the city,
And I'd fallen in love before.
There's something about it that feeds
Even when it's not eaten,
It's the way the sun shines, angles off the cap,
It's the remedy for the lonely evenings with
Nothing but the radio playing love songs.

I don't know anything about him,
Except that he knows the earth, and
Wears a hat to keep the sun off his face, and his jeans
Are dusted like mine. He shows the children
Where the best strawberries grow and how
To pick them, to lift under the belly and
Gently remove the stem, to eat it right away.

Breakfast

I tell myself
        It will be fine
I tell myself
        I don't need you

There is plenty of ocean
There are plenty of stars

        But it has been some years
Since I was loved

        And this morning
When I went out walking

A mountain lion
    Came from behind the trees

And ate my heart

Chocolate

The chocolate sits on the counter
Waiting to be picked up
It wants to
Melt

Dog Park Romance

They run circles around each other
And roll over in the grass
They have their own diplomacy,
Its not all raw, unchecked romping,
There is a decorum in the way they
Lift their leg in just the same spot.

It is almost the witching hour, the magic hour,
Children play hot lava on the play structure
And the dogs bark and jump and sniff, unabashed
With each other, while their owners make small talk,
Socialize more intimately than the lone mothers and fathers
On their Smartphones, *watching* their children play.

The dogs bring us together. The way they chase
Each other is an opener, a conversation starter,
A connection otherwise not imagined.
It's the little interactions that nourish,
And the children are happy playing,
And there's no one to go home to.

Soviet Delicacy

You peeled back the lid of the tin and scooped out a spoonful
Of gelatinous pigeon meat,
Placed it upon the brown napkin like giving alms.

I received it graciously, but when you turned away
I folded the paper around the soft meat and slid it into my pocket.

Something in me would not let it melt upon my tongue,
Like the something in me that evaded
Your touch when you leaned in, too close.
Was it really pigeon meat,

The dance of unknown flavors crushed and damp
Within my jeans? It sat there for a long time,
The bus jostling us along toward The Black Sea.

You'd meant it as a gift, a sharing from the heart.
I could have popped it into my mouth,
Relishing the flavor, the viscous texture,
I could have returned your wink.

Safer in my pocket, un-tasted.
The something in me might have evaporated with
Its consumption, leaving all that is underneath exposed.

Still I wonder, what if the pleasure on your face
Had been worth the taste of pigeon meat?

The Ox and the Dragon

There are twelve spokes on the wheel,
    Each one has its place

The dragon is a creature of fire,
    Dangerous. The Ox does not want
To be consumed, he is stubborn,
    Meaty, earthbound.
The dragon is dazzling and playful,
    She might take flight

The momentum of the circle is
    Movement in every direction,
        Freedom in form

The points do not reach for each other,
    Only dance at angles

She admires his stealth,
    But a dragon could eat an ox for lunch,
        No wonder he is afraid

Limerence

I had a love affair
In my imagination

In the mornings
I would lay my head
On his chest, and stroke the
Three heads of the dragon
Tattoo that wrapped itself
Around his body

I would speak to each one,
Their tongues all a-flame,
And he would run his fingers
Softly through my hair

We would lie there together
In company

Clean Gone

The day he shaved her head it was raining. She watched her
Identity fall to the floor in quick cascades; amber clumps that
Fell gracefully, submissively startled away from her skull, tossed off
Like a piece of clothing. She listened to his encouraging voice, insisting
That "It looks so good…" and squinting, tried to match his words with
The image in the mirror.

It was true she had mentioned to him that she might cut it all off, but she
Was not prepared for the brightness of irrevocable decision.
She placed her head before his razor as if it were a
Block of wood he could now carve to his desired shape. At first
She had said, "No, not today." He responded, "But I have the razor,
Right here in my hand, posed for your slaying." She said, "Okay,
Not to the skin, leave an inch or two." He said, "It's easier to just shave it."
She let herself empty her mind, shrug her shoulders,
As if it didn't really concern her.

And now in her awkwardness she wanders among so many
Metropolitan beauties, feeling like a dull knife among
All these polished swords.
The trees are all flaming red and yellow this time of year,
As if just before they fall they lambent the revelation that
Love was just a passing face.

Uncertainty is not something with which we are born, she thinks,
We are taught it very lovingly. Here, in the city,
People look at each other with candid innocence and say,
"I am clay, mold me," forgetting to shape themselves.

Like the Sun and Moon We Both Can Shine

Last night as you lay dreaming I whispered in your ear
That as often as I come to you will I disappear,
The longer we're together will we later be apart
As much as I thrill you will I disappoint. As much
As I give to you will I take away, as much as there's
Pleasure there will be pain,

You said you needed some time to catch
Your dreams, to seek and find.
And so I let you go, to let you be free,
I knew you'd not forget to remember me.
But when I put on my own set of wings
You pulled me back and said you still needed me.

Now I have wept and I have grieved,
And my newfound self I have received.
And like the sun and moon we both can shine,
And love each other in another time.
My mind is quiet now, my heart is strong,
And so I take my leave and I leave you this song.

Oliver

I went for ride with Oliver Sacks
On his BMW R60,
He did not recognize my face,
But I sang him a Bach Cantata,
So he put up with me for an hour.

We stopped at a nursing home, where
Catatonic inmates came out of their sleep, for a while,
He showed me how the fern reaches
Like a dendrite towards its neighbor,
He noted my nervous tics.

We went to his hotel, where he kept
An octopus in the bathtub,
Lifted barbells in the weight room, and wrote letters
In response to the legion he had received,
My letter never arrived, so I wrote him this poem.

He spouted much less nonsense than any man I've ever known,
Was immensely generous with his gift, that ability to observe and
Discern and accept the complexities and perplexities of life,
Reveled in the discovery of surprise,
Honored experience above erudite conclusions.

My hero is dead,
But halleluiah for the life that he lived.
And watch him now, as he rides off across the Mohabi dessert,
He is smiling. That trip, man,
It was an awakening.

Goethe's Theory of Color

It is when the light is fading that the colors rise,
Orange, salmon, green,
All day the sky is blue, waiting to be revealed

Only clouds enrich the colors
In a storm of silver, smoke
And yellow

Newton had it wrong.
It is when the light disappears
That the colors come out to play

For "color itself is a degree of
Darkness," an opportunity to
Wrestle with the opposite

It is not so much the light that illuminates
The dark, but rather the dark
That enlivens the light

Secrets of the Skeleton

Notice how the sphenoid arches like a butterfly, suspended
Across the cranial vault in graceful flight, it glides
With the subtlest of movements, and the carpals and metacarpals
Curl to meet each other, little diaphragms of cooperation,
The things our hands can do.

Notice the way the pelvic girdle rests like a chalice, how the
Paired bones mirror each other—
How the sutures impress us with their coarseness
While they breathe, —Notice the hyoid bone,
Anchoring above and below, holding us all together.

The vertebrae stacked one on top of the other,
Two perfect scales, the ribs tuning forks,
The spinal membranes: dura, arachnoid, pia,
Threaded like an elaborate, tethered web enshrouding
The spinal cord, all mystery—

The femur producing blood cells, stem cells:
Living tissue strong enough to bear our weight,
The little orchestra of ossicles and tympani orienting
Our place in space, our bodies in time.

Palpate the tension of the fascia
As it winds from bregma to toe,
One continuous and ephemeral manifestation
Of becoming and grace,
These walking temples of bone and water
And ancient memory.

The Way the Wind Sounds

There is an orange-red crackling accompanying great
Gusting whirls, circle dancing, *Whosh-whooo,*
And the sky is a pale yellow ebbing
Into gray-blues, a perfect water-color
But for the breeze, the way the wind sounds when
You trample through the flood of browns and soft yellows.
Autumn the color of dying,
The flame before the trail of smoke that is only
A remembrance of that last walk together,
Before the fire in you died and you were only a haunting,
Color burned into a photograph.
Now the sound is like a sudden waking from sleep,
A trick of the imagination;
The suggestion that if I turn quickly enough, I just might see you
Standing there, trampling leaves as if you'd never passed.

Sailor Man

Well my father was a good ol' man, and a good ol' man was he
He traveled off the beaten path and wandered wild and free
One day he chose to take a wife and had a child, 'twas me
His wanderin' ceased but ne'er his tales as he sat me upon his knee

One tale he spun so full of life, I thought that it was true
Of a sailor and his pretty maid sailing on the ocean blue
A storm blew down and knocked them round upon the waves of salt
Then a bird took flight in the morning light and broke right into song

The maid looked 'round for her sailor man but he was not in sight
Her tears did flow for the bird did tell of a dolphin and his plight
She saw him try to save the man all in the storming sea, but the
Waves were strong and the winds were long, underwater now was he

The maid she sailed back to the land and wandered far and wide
Her grief was great but 'twas her fate to have a husband at her side
She loved him well and ne'er did tell of the ghost of her early love
But he knew her heart was cleft in two at the sight of the turtledove

My father sang this woeful tune with a look all in his eye
As if he'd known the dying man but had never said goodbye
He told me ne'er to give my love to a man upon the sea
Yes, my father was a good ol' man and a good ol' man was he

Flame in Seed

Yesterday, your leaves were still cupped
Like a chrysalis round a butterfly.
This morning you opened your wings,
An eruption of crimson and orange.

When I left you, you turned once more to the white wall.
There was little to see there, but it was your only view.
For a time we chatted, as if everyday small talk
Was all you needed, as if I would be there again tomorrow.

For one full day you radiate, all eyes drawn towards your brilliance,
Green calyx bent down like tiny soldiers bowing at your passing.
They fold before you, as flame reaching towards light,
You open to the sun.

Since you were a young boy the statistics have weighed against
The lingering of a heart's beat that was not predicted to persevere,
So great a hole was to be mended, so intangible was the error,
Surgery could not mend the greater gap.

The creases in your petals make you no less
Beautiful, only more common.
You droop, you bend, your petals fall away,
The seed that encases your next incarnation loosens,
And once more the calyx gives birth.

Memory is a funny thing.
There are places where the sadness was not,
There are moments that will return in retrospection.
There will be other opportunities for emancipation.

The seed will stay in the earth, and with the great effort
Of sunlight and water, wind and toil, it will germinate into a new
Generation of glory. Someone will witness it, be it you or me,
Be it someone not yet open to the sun.

Artificial Light

He spends most of his days now under slightly soiled sheets, a television
Blaring in front of his catatonic neighbor, whose silent protestations
Remain unheard by nurse or visiting nephew,
Curled up inside his paralyzed tongue like a burst of pollen
Waiting to explode, paused by an early frost.

The man in bed 251 B has fewer visitors, his children grown and living
Far away, he mostly stares at the wall, avoids the 5x8 color photograph of
His grandson, too painful to recall a life beyond white walls, disinfectant,
Indistinguishable meals served on a plastic trays five minutes before
The same three hours, three times every day.

The nurses encourage him in sharp falsettos to get out of bed,
Stretch his legs, but the Patio is full of smokers, something he can't abide.
He might hazily recall the feel of sunlight, the scent of a summer
Breeze wafting across the Louisiana bayou,
Perhaps the sound of a bird's call,
But there is no window in this room out of which to gaze,
Not at the sun or starlight, or to listen to the traffic or the wind.

In his previous life he was a busy man, worked nine to five,
Raised children, listened to Louis Armstrong and Bob Dylan,
Had good taste. Wore a belt. Shoes. Did the little things for himself
That he's now forgotten how to perform, as if his fingers had lost their
Meaning under fluorescent lights, among pill-dispensing nurses
Almost always smiling.

He is silent now, although his daughter calls him once a week,
Just to check in, to make small talk, ease her conscience.
This man who's being has somehow dispersed, though his body goes on
And on, heart beating with a displaced rhythm,
A muffled beat terrified of being overheard, yet grievously wishing
For another chance, if only one morning upon waking
His eyes could open and see something besides white walls.

Skylark

When my daughter didn't speak
I rose up like the ocean sends a wave
To wash out all the silence;
When people asked, I explained
"She's shy," my hand shrouding her
Head pressed against my thigh.

I would imagine her voice like roses
Whispering secrets;
One must listen carefully in a garden.
What she had to say
Took flight with her hands,
Like birds singing.

They sang, they told, they spoke,
Her eyes accompanied,
And I did not demand a timber.
When she laughed one day
It was like a church bell ringing,
The sound of a skylark.

The Heart Is Not a Pump

1.

He slit open the pericardium first,
The protective layer like a fitted glove,
So thin, but stronger than you'd think.

They say the heart is not a pump.
It is the blood that moves it,
It is the will that pulses even while
It aches. Broken cord or not,
The heart is a muscle.

2.

She lay on the table, cold metal,
There was a stillness past sleep.

We gathered round her, and he
Took the scalpel and cut into her chest,
A perfect six-inch slit that opened onto fat and
Fascia; pulling back the nerves and bone,
It was the heart we were digging for.

It was given its own tray, like a gift,
But for the thickness of the blood, it looked
Like it might still beat.

3.

There is a force we haven't named.
And the textbooks are all wrong, if you study physics.
Blood flows in a spiral. The heart is the epicenter,
But it is the breath that makes it pulse.
It is the blood that moves it to dance.

Playing Chopin

If my fingers didn't remember the lugubrious chords,
My heart would, they are both
Just muscle memory

Thank God for Chopin,

He takes me up into his doleful hands and
Plays me with so much more depth
Than you did

The Sunflower Is a Twelve-pointed Star

They talk about love as if it could be
  Contained,
As if it didn't permeate
  Everything
The lies they tell cast
  Shadows,
They darken the sky

When something is
  Shattered
It cannot be fitted back together like
  puzzle pieces,
It can only rise from ashes,
  Transformed

The light is beautiful,
  It scrapes,
Like shards of glass prickling the skin,
  Illuminating little holes
In our perception, revealing
The stains and blotches and gaps that
  Speckled our failing.

In its brightness
  We are left with a tangled jumble
Of Memories, we are left with nothing
  But ourselves.

The circle completes itself
  In twelve arcs,
The light gleams through,
And sun mirroring sun, it
  Reaches

Loss

Child of light, forgive me,
Even your mother cannot forge this
Broken metal

—can only be one half
Of your beginning,
—cannot fill your longing
Or offer balm to soothe your
Heartache
        —he left me, too

—cannot even shepherd you through the cleft,
For I am only the wall you lean against

Malignancy

You thought you were just doing
Your job, quietly building
Little cities in the valley of my throat,
Stringing electric lights meant to
Wake me up with their zing.

I am awake.
I am listening to the whir
Of your rattle.
My soul is sparkling; *body,*
Won't you cooperate?

Release your chokehold,
Loosen your grip, your
Claws like a cat kneading circles.

I will undo them one by one, those claws,
Until there is nothing left but a
Memory of pain, and in place of the
Black growth,
Little droplets of bright red
Blood flowering.

One Was Not Enough

He was honest about it from the start.
I will love you, but I will love her, too.
    And maybe her.

It was hard in between not to want
    More of him,
Every time after she wanted less of the want.

Sex is not unburdened,
    It is not pure,
There is the ebb and flow of give and take
And need and want and claim,
    There's the exchange.

Each one of us thinks perhaps
    I will be enough
But it is not true,
And he is honest about it from the start.

We are all at odds within ourselves,
Claiming the same freedom,
Yet always wanting more.

Yet part of the act of intimacy is
Staking a claim, opening a door,
Taking something in return,
Love may be free, but sex
Is bound by the body.

I'll embody the challenge, to see if I
Can love so freely, to see if there really is
More love when you love more, less.

And it's okay to share,
Because how greedy can you be?

The Orange Clawfoot Bathtub

It sat in the hot expanse
Of the attic, like a boat
Tethered in the shallows.

The white porcelain interior cool,
Like a basin of water,
The promise
Of baptism contained in its kiss.

I want to lie down in the sun,
Bask in its marigold warmth,
To sit in its porcelain lap,
And shine.

Orange is the moment,
Freedom standing on the abyss,
A sparkling in the light.

Lover's Point

Love is a more expansive thing than it used to be.
There is no possessiveness, no ball and chain.
It wears wings and sturdy boots, walks untethered,
Envelopes and permeates and breathes.

After I saw you, I went to the garden.
Two butterflies danced in circles around me,
Alighting on one another's backs,
They flew off into the sun.

Later, you walked with me to lover's point,
Showed me its cliff edges and soft grass,
It's apples, and the moments that are like diamonds,
You lay me down in the grass and
Almost came near enough to touch.

My body does not know
Anything but that your touch is good.
My ears do not know anything
But that the music of your laughter is
Music that I want to hear.

There is no need for explanations.
I have enough heart to swallow the conditions,
To accept the take it or leave it envelope of
This is the way it is.
There is only the moment, the grace of
The everlasting now that carries us
To the next flight.

Aurore Sibley lives in the San Francisco Bay Area with her two children. She is an education specialist with a background in the healing arts, a performing musician, and somehow finds time to write essays, poetry and short stories in her spare time. She believes that the arts and sciences are more closely connected than is generally warranted.

Her writing has appeared in various journalistic publications, including *Lilipoh* magazine and *The Idea Crucible*. This is her first collection of poetry.

www.ingramcontent.com/pod-product-compliance
Lightning Source LLC
LaVergne TN
LVHW041520070426
835507LV00012B/1710